MIXOLOGY

How to Be the Drink Mixer in Your Crowd

HOTEL *Jordan* TAP ROOM • GLENDIVE, MONTANA

MIXOLOGY

How to Be the Drink Mixer in Your Crowd

HOLLY RAPPORT

WARNER BOOKS

NEW YORK   BOSTON

Postcard Images: Found Image Press

Illustrations by Milan Bozic

Designed by Leah Lococo Ltd

Time Warner Book Group

1271 Avenue of the Americas, New York, N.Y. 10020

Visit our Web site at www.twbookmark.com

First Edition: July 2005

10 9 8 7 6 5 4 3 2 1

LCCN: 2004114163

ISBN: 0-446-69526-2

TWP

Printed in Singapore

ACKNOWLEDGMENTS

First and foremost, I want to thank Stacey Ashton, my publisher, friend, and great drinking buddy. This book would have never happened without your vision, and I thank you for inviting me to be a part of it. You're the best!

To all of my drinking buddies (you know who you are), thank you for helping me with years of research. To Yosh, you are always there for me, especially for a ski-break cocktail. Many thanks to Jean Griffin (for hiring me!) and Olga Vezeris, my editor and cheerleader, of Time Warner Book Group.

This book is dedicated to my father, who has stood by me with endless support and love, through good times and bad. I love you Dad. And to my mother, who is always in my heart, and who, as an avid reader, would be proud that I got published.

CONTENTS

Whiskey ▪ 41

Algonquin ❋ Canadian Cocktail ❋ Irish Coffee ❋ Manhattan
Manhattan (Dry) ❋ Old-Fashioned ❋ Ward Eight ❋ Whiskey Sour

Scotch ▪ 47

Godfather ❋ Rob Roy ❋ Rusty Nail

Bourbon ▪ 51

Bourbon Cobbler ❋ Chapel Hill ❋ Kentucky Cocktail ❋ Louisville Cooler ❋ Mint Julep

Rum ▪ 57

Bacardi Cocktail ❋ Beachcomber ❋ Continental ❋ Cuba Libre
Cuban Cocktail ❋ Daiquiri ❋ Hurricane ❋ Mai Tai ❋ Piña Colada
Planter's Punch ❋ XYZ ❋ Zombie

Brandy ▪ 65

Apricot Cocktail ❋ Bombay Cocktail ❋ Bosom Caresser
Brandy Alexander ❋ Brandy Crusta Cocktail ❋ Deauville Cocktail ❋ East India Cocktail
Jack Rose Cocktail ❋ Royal Smile Cocktail ❋ Sidecar ❋ Stinger
Third Rail ❋ Whip Cocktail ❋ Widow's Kiss

Tequila ▪ 71

Brave Bull ❋ Margarita ❋ Matador ❋ Shady Lady ❋ Silk Stockings
Tequila Sunrise ❋ Toreador ❋ Viva Villa

INTRODUCTION

January 16, 1920 (the other "D day"). A date all drinkers would like to forget . . . the day Prohibition began. The good news is that Prohibition was not the living hell that all cocktail lovers feared—in truth, the Roaring Twenties was a wonderful time in America, a time when Americans learned to truly love the art of imbibing.

During the '20s many of the great cocktails were born: the Sidecar, Bloody Mary, Bronx Cocktail, Martini. There is a reason that these classics have endured—they are great drinks! Retro drinks are in style for every generation because they never go out of style.

The popularity of the cocktail flourished in the '30s and '40s, and especially in the '50s. After the Great Depression, Americans had a lot to toast and celebrate! Cocktail parties—in full swing in the '50s—were a great time to bring together friends and acquaintances in a fun, social atmosphere.

The '60s were a dark time for cocktails—they were considered too "establishment" and therefore not cool. To be rebellious was not to have a three-martini lunch. The counterculture was more interested in smoking marijuana and dropping acid than in mixing cocktails. The decade of the '70s, with its flamboyance and disco-trashy vibes, and the conservative Reagan-era '80s were not times for a cocktail comeback either.

Fortunately (finally!), in the mid-'90s, the cocktail made a huge reentry into popular culture, with the reemergence of the most classic cocktail of them all: the martini. There was a conscious nostalgia about the new retro craze, as though hipsters were deliberately trying to be rat packers, dancing to nuevo swing dance music, smoking cigars, and drinking new-style martinis. There was no shame in embracing all things retro; even popular culture played along, with the *Austin Powers* and *Swingers* movies, *Sex and the City* television show, and the popularity of lounges and swing dancing.

In the twenty-first century we continue to embrace retro cocktails. There is something eternally glamorous about ordering a classic drink that comes delivered in a beautiful glass with a garnish. And entertaining friends, acquaintances, and colleagues in your home by serving fabulous drinks will make you the master drink mixer in your crowd. Mixology is not an exact science, which is why anyone can do it. That's the fun aspect of hosting a soirée in your home—you can experiment with ingredients, have theme parties, and become even more popular.

I hope you enjoy this book as much as I enjoyed researching and writing it. The key to a successful cocktail party is to know your guests' tastes and to never run out of ice or alcohol. Drinks in this book are on the stronger side, so be sure to change the ingredient amounts to please your palate. Be creative with your cocktails. As long as you keep your guests' preferences in mind, your parties will be a success.

Mixology: It's an Art

There really *is* an art of preparing mixed drinks. In this book you'll learn what you need to know to be a successful bartender and cocktail party host or hostess. Every home bartender should know

and practice mixology—it comes down to having the right bar tools (or the right substitutes), the freshest ingredients, a stocked bar, and the desire to serve the best and most delicious drinks possible. Making a good mixed drink for your guests just takes some practice, and, these pointers will help:

* Use a shot glass (measure or jigger) to measure the correct amount of alcohol for each drink.
* Chill your cocktail glasses.
* Refrigerate mixers before using; mixers should be cold, not room temperature.
* Serve a decent variety of cocktails to your guests. Remember not everyone drinks rum, some people can't stomach tequila, others like frozen drinks, etc.
* Try your best never to run out of ice (have extra on hand just in case).
* Have fun! Your guests will have more fun if you do.

Stocking the Bar: What You'll Need

It would be nice to have one of everything stocked in your home bar. It's hard enough to remember to buy milk sometimes! Therefore, have available what you like to drink and what you like to serve—and fill in the gaps for special occasions, like the theme parties listed at the end of this book (see page 89).

SPIRITS & WINES

This is an "essentials" list; add your favorite spirits to it as well. Note: vodka should be kept in the freezer, and white wine should be refrigerated. Top-shelf liquor is more expensive, but you suffer fewer and less-horrible hangovers later. It's worth it just for that! Indulge your guests and go for the good stuff.

* Bourbon
* Brandy
* Champagne
* Gin
* Liqueurs
* Rum
* Scotch
* Sherry
* Tequila
* Vermouth
  (dry and sweet)
* Vodka
* Whiskey
* Wine (red and white)

MIXERS

As noted earlier, mixers should always be refrigerated. I emphasize using fresh juices instead of canned or bottled, as fresh always tastes best.

* Club Soda
* Cola (diet and regular)
* Cranberry Juice
* Cream (light cream or half-half)
* Ginger Ale
* Grapefruit Juice
* Lemon Juice
* Lime Juice
* Orange Juice
* Pineapple Juice
* Tomato Juice
* Tonic Water

GARNISHES & CONDIMENTS

The following ingredients are very important to a drink's outcome; therefore, use the best you can afford. Remember: presentation is important with cocktails! Classic cocktails always have great colorful garnishes—carry on this wonderful tradition in your own home. And feel free to be creative with your retro cocktails—use little umbrellas to accent your Mai Tais, or put strawberries in your Manhattans.

This is a longish list of what you'll need; you

can always use what you have at home to substitute if you must. Fresh fruit should always be used if possible; if it isn't, canned is an OK substitute (it's also quicker if you're out of time!). When planning your party, make sure not to cut your fruit garnishes too early (they'll dry out). A few hours before the party will be fine.

- ✻ Bananas
- ✻ Bitters
- ✻ Black Pepper
- ✻ Celery
- ✻ Cinnamon Sticks
- ✻ Coarse Salt
- ✻ Cocktail Olives
- ✻ Grenadine
- ✻ Horseradish
- ✻ Lemons
- ✻ Limes
- ✻ Maraschino Cherries
- ✻ Milk
- ✻ Mint (fresh)
- ✻ Nutmeg (ground)
- ✻ Oranges
- ✻ Orgeat Syrup (almond-flavored syrup)
- ✻ Pineapples
- ✻ Strawberries
- ✻ Sugar (powdered and granulated)
- ✻ Tabasco Sauce

Glassware: Fill 'Em Up

The following glassware is recommended for your bar. Serving a drink in the proper glass enhances presentation. However, you can always use glasses you already own or plastic cups. Unfortunately with plastic cups you won't have that wonderful sound of ice clinking against glass that adds a classy touch to the party ambiance . . . so try your best to at least have some glassware on hand.

- ✻ Brandy Snifter
- ✻ Champagne Flute
- ✻ Cocktail
- ✻ Collins
- ✻ Cordial
- ✻ Highball
- ✻ Hurricane
- ✻ Irish Coffee
- ✻ Margarita
- ✻ Old-fashioned
- ✻ Shot
- ✻ Sour
- ✻ Red Wine
- ✻ White Wine

Measuring Tools and Terms: Size It Up

Every home bar needs the right equipment to get the job done. The following are the basics; if you can swing it, it's also helpful (and, again, enhances presentation) to have an ice bucket with tongs, a punch bowl, and a glass pitcher. A citrus juicer is wonderful to own for fresh juicing (a perfect gift for your next birthday!). Stock up on toothpicks, straws, and swizzle sticks. For an elegant touch, get some fancy cocktail napkins and retro coasters to add to the atmosphere.

❋ Bar Spoon (long-handled spoon for mixing)

❋ Blender

❋ Bottle Opener

❋ Can Opener

❋ Cocktail Shaker

❋ Corkscrew

❋ Jigger (aka measure or shot glass)

❋ Measuring Cup (for liquids)

❋ Measuring Spoons

❋ Mixing Glass

❋ Muddler for mashing ingredients together (or you can always use the back of a spoon to muddle)

❋ Paring Knife

❋ Strainer

MEASUREMENT CHART

It is worth taking the time to measure all of your ingredients when preparing mixed drinks. If you don't, you risk ruining a drink's taste, and that is certainly not worth it. So, slow down, measure, and get better results.

1 cup	8 ounces
1 dash	$1/32$ ounce
1 jigger	$1 1/2$ ounces
1 pony	1 ounce
1 splash	$1/2$ ounce
1 teaspoon	$1/8$ ounce
1 tablespoon	$3/8$ ounce
1 wineglass	4 ounces

Useful Tips for the Future Cocktail Connoisseur: A How-to-Do

There are certain bartender skills to learn before you get a party started.

HOW TO CHILL A GLASS

Serving cocktails in chilled glasses is the way to go—it adds to the presentation of the drink and gives it an extra cold edge. These are some ways to chill a glass:

❄ For extra frosty glassware, dip the glass in cold water, shake it off, and put it in the freezer.

❄ Put the glass in the freezer (10 minutes) or in the refrigerator (30+ minutes).

❄ Quick-time method: pack a tall glass (a highball or collins) with ice and let it stand for at least 5 minutes. For a cocktail glass, fill it with ice and pour water over it and let it stand. Dump the ice out of the glass, shake off excess water and add the mixed drink immediately.

Note: always use fresh ice in a drink, i.e., always dump out the ice you use to chill a glass before adding the mixed drink.

HOW TO SUGAR/SALT A RIM

Some drinks will require you to coat the rim of the glass. Chill the glass first and then dip the rim of the glass in water to wet it (or you can wet the rim with fresh lemon or lime juice). Pour sugar or salt onto a plate (make sure it's spread out to fit the glass), then dip the rim into the sugar or salt. For a margarita, wet the rim of the margarita glass with a lime wedge or juice, then dip the rim into coarse salt.

HOW TO PREPARE A GARNISH

The time to prepare a garnish is right before using it so that it is as fresh as possible. If you are planning a party and need lots of garnishes, prepare them a few hours beforehand and store them covered in the refrigerator.

Fruit Garnishes

Again, fresh fruit is the best. Wash the peel of citrus fruits (lemons, limes, and oranges) before cutting; other fruits can be peeled (bananas).

Twist: Cut the fruit at both ends (or in half lengthwise, which may be easier) and scoop out the inside with a spoon. With either a sharp paring knife or vegetable peeler, cut the peel lengthwise into thin strips about 1 1/2" long and 3/8" wide. For garnishing, twist the peel over the cocktail to release the fruit's oil, and drop it into the drink.

Lemon and Lime: For garnishing with slices of lemon or lime, cut the fruit in half lengthwise, then slice into wedges to be squeezed into the cocktail. Remove any seeds and pith from the wedges before using.

Olives: Use stuffed olives and spear them with wooden toothpicks.

Cocktail Onions: Prepare the same as you would olives.

HOW TO SERVE ICE

Ice is as important to your party as having the right alcohol and glasses. You must make your best effort to never run out of ice, as this will result in someone having to go out and fetch some more. This is bad party etiquette and should be avoided! Make sure your ice is clean and fresh. Buy ice cubes or make them yourself for highball cocktails, old-fashioneds, and any on-the-rocks drinks that your guests may prefer. For any drinks you will be shaking or stirring, use cracked ice or cubes. To crush cubes at home, put some cubes into a plastic bag and pound with a hammer.

The most glamorous way to serve ice at your party is with an ice bucket and tongs. Using tongs instead of a spoon to serve ice is much easier, and your guests will thank you for sparing them the embarrassment of losing ice cubes to the floor.

HOW TO SHAKE & STIR

There are some traditional methods: shake drinks made with creams, sugar, and juices; stir drinks made of clear ingredients.

To shake: Fill a shaker (about two-thirds full) with ice, then add the drink ingredients. Ice first before ingredients, as the ice will quickly cool the shaker. Cover the shaker and shake it up. Strain the ingredients into a glass.

To stir: Add ice and the drink ingredients (ice first!) to a mixing glass (you can also stir in the drink glass, or in a shaker as well) and stir vigorously with a bar spoon.

HOW TO MUDDLE

Muddling is mashing ingredients (such as mint) in the bottom of a glass. You can use either a wooden muddler or the back of a spoon.

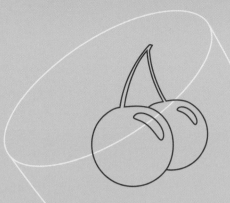

You don't have to drink alone!
The Ultimate Classic Cocktail Movies:

1. *Casablanca*
2. *Breakfast at Tiffany's*
3. *Ocean's Eleven* (the 1960 version)
4. *Harvey*
5. *Arthur*
6. *Adam's Rib*
7. *All About Eve*
8. *Goldfinger*
9. *The Thin Man*
10. *The Great Gatsby*
11. *To Have and Have Not*
12. *Sabrina*

CROYDON COCKTAIL
CIRCLE
614
RUSH
STREET
CHICAGO

Let's start with America's favorite spirit: vodka. The craze for vodka started with the Russian-made Smirnoff mixed with ginger beer and lime, the drink known as the Moscow Mule. By the 1960s vodka had surpassed its elder, gin, in popularity and folks were following James Bond's lead by using vodka in their martinis, instead of the usual gin. Most often vodka is distilled from grain or potatoes, and it's always odorless and it used to be always colorless. These days, there are many popular colored and flavored vodkas to choose from. (Many are featured in the *New Retro Martinis* chapter of this book.) Because of its traditional look and smell, vodka has a wonderful way of blending with whatever you mix it with—sweet, sour, or otherwise. Some of the all-time favorite retro drinks are vodka-based: the Bloody Mary, Salty Dog, and White Russian, to name a few. Vodka doesn't have 20 percent of the American market share for nothing!

Bikini

2 oz. Vodka

1 oz. Light Rum

1/2 oz. Milk

1 tsp. Sugar

1 spritz Lemon Juice

Combine ingredients in shaker with ice.
Shake, then strain into chilled cocktail glass.
Garnish: lemon twist

Black Russian

1 1/2 oz. Vodka

3/4 oz. Kahlúa

Combine ingredients in shaker with ice, shake,
then pour into old-fashioned glass.

Bloody Mary

1 1/2 oz. Vodka

3 oz. Tomato Juice

1/2 tsp. Worcestershire Sauce

1 tsp. Lemon Juice

2–3 drops Tabasco Sauce

Ground Black Pepper to taste

Combine ingredients in shaker with ice,
shake, then strain into highball glass over ice.
Garnish: celery stick or lime wedge

Bull Shot

2 oz. Vodka

4 oz. Chilled Beef Bouillon

1/2 tsp. Worcestershire Sauce

Salt and Pepper to taste

Combine ingredients in shaker with ice, shake,
then strain into old-fashioned glass.

Cape Codder

2 oz. Vodka

5 oz. Cranberry Juice

Combine ingredients in mixing glass with ice and stir. Strain into ice-filled highball glass.

Garnish: lime wedge

Harvey Wallbanger

1 1/2 oz. Vodka

4 oz. Orange Juice

1/2 oz. Galliano

Combine vodka and orange juice in mixing glass with ice and stir. Strain into ice-filled collins glass. Float Galliano on top.

Garnish: cherry and orange slice

Madras

2 oz. Vodka

4 oz. Cranberry Juice

2 oz. Orange Juice

Combine ingredients in mixing glass with ice. Stir, then strain into ice-filled highball glass.

Garnish: lime wedge

Moscow Mule

2 oz. Vodka

Ginger Beer

1 tsp. Lime Juice

Combine vodka and lime juice in mixing glass with ice. Stir, then strain into ice-filled collins glass, and fill with ginger beer.

Garnish: lime wedge

Pink Lemonade

2 oz. Vodka

3/4 oz. Triple Sec

1/2 oz. Lime Juice

1 oz. Sour Mix

2 oz. Cranberry Juice

Combine ingredients in shaker with ice.

Shake, then strain into ice-filled collins glass.

Garnish: lemon wheel

Russian Cocktail

1 oz. Vodka

1 oz. Crème de Cacao (white)

1 oz. Gin

Combine ingredients in shaker with ice, shake, then strain into chilled cocktail glass.

Salty Dog

2 oz. Vodka

5 oz. Grapefruit Juice

1 tsp. Salt

Combine ingredients in mixing glass with ice. Stir, then strain into ice-filled highball glass. *Garnish*: lime wedge

Screwdriver

2 oz. Vodka

5 oz. Orange Juice

Combine ingredients in mixing glass with ice. Stir, then strain into ice-filled highball glass. *Garnish*: orange slice

Velvet Hammer

1 1/2 oz. Vodka

1/2 oz. Crème de Cacao (white)

1/2 oz. Light Cream

Combine ingredients in shaker with ice, shake, then strain into chilled cocktail glass.

White Russian

2 oz. Vodka

1 oz. Kahlúa

1 oz. Light Cream

Combine vodka and Kahlúa in ice-filled old-fashioned glass. Fill with cream.

The main ingredient for the classiest classic cocktail of them all (the martini, of course!) was originally created in the seventeenth century for medicinal purposes. The inventor, a Dutch native named Dr. Sylvius, had the right idea—gin does have special "restorative" powers; as people back in the old days drank gin to cure all of their "health" problems. (It helps when you're drunk enough not to remember your problems.) Gin is distilled from grain and flavored primarily with juniper berries. Angelica, orange peel, coriander, and other spices and herbs are also used for flavor. Gin is very often associated with Prohibition, as bathtub gin was made in the United States illegally and was the easiest liquor to manufacture. The martini, stirred not shaken, is the ultimate gin cocktail—and became even more notorious with 007 James "shaken not stirred" Bond. Probably not getting the kudos they deserve are the other classic gin cocktails, including the Gin Rickey, Gimlet, Singapore Sling, and Tom Collins.

Aviation

1 1/2 oz. Gin

3/4 Maraschino Liqueur

1 tsp. Lemon Juice

Combine ingredients in shaker with ice,
shake, then strain into chilled cocktail glass.
Garnish: lemon twist or cherry

Bronx Cocktail

1 oz. Gin

1/2 oz. Dry Vermouth

1/2 oz. Sweet Vermouth

1/2 oz. Orange Juice

Combine ingredients in shaker with ice,
shake, then strain into chilled cocktail glass.
Garnish: orange slice

Darb Cocktail

1 oz. Gin

1 oz. Dry Vermouth

1 oz. Apricot-flavored Brandy

1 tsp. Lemon Juice

Combine ingredients in shaker with ice,
shake, then strain into chilled cocktail glass.
Garnish: lemon twist

Gibson

2 oz. Gin

1 tsp. Dry Vermouth

Combine ingredients in mixing glass with ice,
stir, then strain into chilled cocktail glass.
Garnish: skewered cocktail onions

Gimlet

2 oz. Gin

1 oz. Lime Juice

Combine ingredients in shaker with ice, shake, then strain into chilled cocktail glass.

Garnish: lime wedge

Gin Cobbler

2 oz. Club Soda

1 tsp. Sugar

2 oz. Gin

Combine club soda and sugar in old-fashioned glass and dissolve. Add gin and ice, then stir. Serve with small straws. *Garnish*: orange slice and cherry

Gin Daisy

2 oz. Gin

1 oz. Lemon Juice

$1/2$ tsp. Grenadine

$1/2$ tsp. Sugar

Combine ingredients in shaker with ice, shake, then strain into ice-filled old-fashioned glass. *Garnish*: orange slice and cherry

Gin Fizz

2 oz. Gin

1 oz. Lemon Juice

1 tsp. Sugar

Club Soda

Combine gin, lemon juice, and sugar in shaker with ice, shake, then strain into ice-filled highball glass. Fill with club soda and stir.

Gin Rickey

$1 1/4$ oz. Gin

1 oz. Lime Juice

Club Soda

Combine gin and lime juice in ice-filled highball glass. Fill with club soda and stir. *Garnish*: lime wedge

Judge Jr. Cocktail

1 oz. Gin

1 oz. Light Rum

$^1/_2$ oz. Lemon Juice

$^3/_4$ tsp. Powdered Sugar

$^1/_2$ tsp. Grenadine

Combine ingredients in a shaker with ice, shake, then strain into cocktail glass.

Martini

2 oz. Gin

$^1/_2$ oz. Vermouth

Combine ingredients in mixing glass with ice, stir, then strain into chilled cocktail glass.

Garnish: skewered olives

Orange Blossom

1 $^1/_4$ oz. Gin

1 oz. Orange Juice

1 tsp. Sugar

Combine ingredients in shaker with ice, shake, then strain into chilled cocktail glass.

Pink Lady

1 $^1/_2$ oz. Gin

1 oz. Light Cream

$^1/_2$ oz. Grenadine

Combine ingredients in shaker with ice, shake, then strain into champagne flute.

Rolls-Royce Martini

2 oz. Gin

1 oz. Dry Vermouth

1 oz. Sweet Vermouth

1 tsp. Benedictine

Combine ingredients in shaker with ice, shake, then strain into chilled cocktail glass.

Singapore Sling

1 1/4 oz. Gin

1 oz. Grenadine

1 oz. Lime Juice

Club Soda

1 oz. Cherry Brandy

Combine gin, grenadine, and lime juice in shaker with ice, shake, then strain into ice-filled collins glass. Fill with club soda and float brandy on top.
Garnish: cherry and orange slice

Tom Collins

2 oz. Gin

1 oz. Sour Mix

Club Soda

Combine gin and sour mix in shaker with ice, shake, then strain into ice-filled collins glass. Fill with club soda and stir. Serve with straw.
Garnish: cherry, orange slice

The "New" Retro
MARTINIS

"I'd like to have a martini

Two at the very most—

After three I'm under the table,

After four I'm under my host."

—Dorothy Parker

A s you know, unless you haven't been to a bar in twenty years, martinis are as popular today as they were back in the '20s. Perhaps the martini's simplicity is its greatest charm, and the key to its enduring popularity. Many purists believe that a martini is *only* gin plus vermouth and an olive. However, and lucky for us, most martini drinkers like to mix it up a bit and try new variations on the old standard. Your martini bar should include martini glasses (cocktail glasses, not plastic, please), a stainless-steel cocktail shaker, cocktail olives, and fresh garnishes.

Specialty martinis became the rage in the '90s, with the popular Cosmopolitan martini at the forefront. Have fun experimenting with the following recipes for some of the most popular "new" retro martinis imbibed today.

Apple Martini

1 oz. Vodka

$^1/_2$ oz. Apple Schnapps

Combine ingredients in mixing glass with ice,
stir, then strain into chilled cocktail glass.

Blue Skyy Martini

$2^1/_2$ oz. Skyy Vodka

$^1/_4$ oz. Blue Curaçao

Combine ingredients in shaker with ice,
shake, then strain into chilled cocktail glass.
Garnish: lemon twist

Chocolate Martini

2 oz. Vodka

$^1/_2$ oz. Chocolate Liqueur

Combine ingredients in mixing glass with ice,
stir, then strain into chilled cocktail glass.

Cosmopolitan

2 oz. Lemon-flavored Vodka

1 oz. Triple Sec

$^1/_2$ oz. Lime Juice

1 oz. Cranberry Juice

Combine ingredients in shaker with ice,
shake, then strain into chilled cocktail glass.

Garnish: lime wedge

Lemon Drop Martini

2 oz. Lemon-flavored Vodka

$^1/_2$ oz. Triple Sec

1 tsp. Sugar

$^3/_4$ oz. Lemon Juice

Combine ingredients in shaker with ice,
shake, then strain into chilled cocktail glass.

Garnish: lemon twist

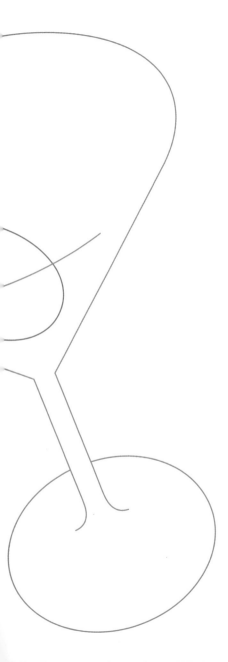

Melon Cocktail

2 oz. Gin

$^1/_2$ oz. Maraschino Liqueur

$^1/_2$ oz. Lemon Juice

Combine ingredients in shaker with ice, shake, then strain into chilled cocktail glass. *Garnish*: maraschino cherry

Metropolitan

2 oz. Brandy

1 oz. Sweet Vermouth

$^1/_2$ tsp. Sugar

1 dash Angostura Bitters

Combine ingredients in shaker with ice, shake, then strain into chilled cocktail glass.

SKY★BAR

Lindsay's

10625
EUCLID AVE.

CLEVELAND
OHIO

THE MOST
UNIQUE AND
COLORFUL
NITE-CLUB
IN TOWN

WHISKEY

From the Algonquin, Old-Fashioned, and timeless Manhattan—whiskey is *the* classic liquor. One can always depend on whiskey to warm the belly on a cold winter's night. Made from grain, a whiskey's flavor and style are determined by several components: the types of yeast used, the method of distilling, the aging processes, and the types of grain (corn, barley, rye, or wheat) in it. Produced mainly in the United States, Canada, Ireland, and Scotland, whiskey is separated into different types, including blended whiskey (one or more straight whiskeys blended together with neutral grain spirits), straight whiskey (aged for at least two years and made from a minimum of 51 percent grain), Irish whiskey (blended), and Canadian whisky (spelled without the "e" and blended).

Algonquin

1 1/2 oz. Blended Whiskey

1 oz. Dry Vermouth

1 oz. Pineapple Juice

Combine ingredients in shaker with ice, shake, then strain into chilled cocktail glass.

Canadian Cocktail

2 oz. Canadian Whisky

1 oz. Triple Sec

1 dash Bitters

1 tsp. Sugar

Combine ingredients in shaker with ice, shake, then strain into chilled cocktail glass.

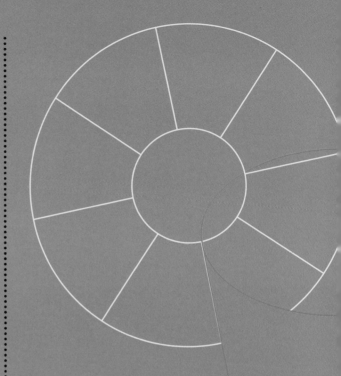

Irish Coffee

1 1/2 oz. Irish Whiskey

Hot Coffee

Whipped Cream

Pour Irish whiskey into Irish coffee glass and add coffee. *Garnish*: whipped cream

Manhattan

2 oz. Whiskey

1 oz. Sweet Vermouth

Combine ingredients in mixing glass with ice, stir, then strain into chilled cocktail glass. *Garnish*: cherry

Manhattan (Dry)

$1^{1}/_{2}$ oz. Whiskey

$^{3}/_{4}$ oz. Dry Vermouth

Combine ingredients in mixing glass with ice, stir, then strain into chilled cocktail glass. *Garnish*: olive

Old-Fashioned

2 dashes Bitters

1 Sugar Cube

$^{1}/_{2}$ oz. Water

3 oz. Blended Whiskey

Muddle bitters, sugar, and water in old-fashioned glass. Add whiskey and crushed ice, then stir. Serve with swizzle stick. *Garnish:* orange slice, twist of lemon, and cherry

Ward Eight

2 oz. Rye Whiskey

1 tsp. Lime Juice

1 tsp. Lemon Juice

1 dash Grenadine

Combine ingredients in shaker with ice, shake, then strain into goblet. *Garnish*: lemon and orange wedges and cherry

Whiskey Sour

2 oz. Blended Whiskey

$^1/_2$ tsp. Sugar

1 oz. Lemon Juice

Combine ingredients in shaker with ice, shake, then strain into sour glass. *Garnish*: cherry and lemon slice

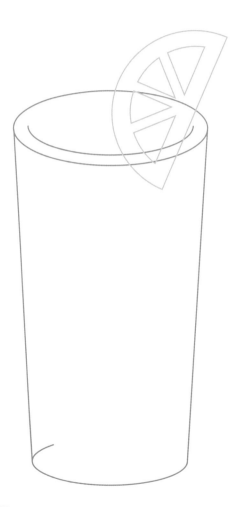

HOTEL *Jordan* TAP ROOM — GLENDIVE, MONTANA

The Scottish are not only recognized for putting men in skirts! They are also known worldwide as the only producers of scotch whisky (no "e" in the name, just like the Canadian). Most scotch is aged at least eight years. There are two primary categories of scotch: blended and single malt. Blended scotch comprises mixed single malts combined with grain whisky—and is the most popular and well-known type of scotch in the United States. Single malt scotch is distilled from malted barley and not blended with any other whiskys. Scotch varies with the different distillers, and the variety depends on aging processes, the kind of water used, distillation techniques, among other things. Delight in these scotch cocktails: Godfather, Rob Roy, Rusty Nail.

Godfather

2 oz. Scotch

1 oz. Amaretto

Combine ingredients in mixing glass with ice and
stir. Strain into ice-filled old-fashioned glass.

Rob Roy

1 ¹/₂ oz. Scotch

³/₄ oz. Sweet Vermouth

Combine ingredients in shaker with ice,
shake, then strain into chilled cocktail glass.
Garnish: cherry

Rusty Nail

2 oz. Scotch

1 oz. Drambuie

Pour scotch into ice-filled old-fashioned glass.
Float Drambuie on top.

BOURBON

Bourbon: The all-American liquor! More than 90 percent of the world's bourbon is produced in Kentucky. This spirit is corn-based whiskey distilled from a mash of grain, and aged in oak barrels for a minimum of two years (it's U.S. law). Additionally, there is a law prohibiting the sale of any foreign-produced bourbon in America. Some call this robust spirit the finest of American whiskeys; enjoy your bourbon in a Mint Julep, Kentucky Cocktail, or on the rocks with a twist.

Bourbon Cobbler

2 $^1\!/_2$ oz. Bourbon

$^1\!/_2$ oz. Grapefruit Juice

$^1\!/_2$ oz. Lemon Juice

2 tsp. Almond Extract

Combine ingredients in mixing glass and stir.
Pour into ice-filled old-fashioned glass.
Garnish: peach slice

Chapel Hill

2 oz. Bourbon

2 oz. Triple Sec

$^1\!/_2$ oz. Lemon Juice

Combine ingredients in shaker with ice,
shake, then strain into chilled cocktail glass.
Garnish: twist of orange peel

Kentucky Cocktail

1 1/2 oz. Bourbon

3/4 oz. Pineapple Juice

Combine ingredients in shaker with ice, shake, then strain into chilled cocktail glass.

Louisville Cooler

2 oz. Bourbon

1/2 oz. Lime Juice

1 oz. Orange Juice

1 tsp. Sugar

Combine ingredients in shaker with ice, shake, then strain into ice-filled old-fashioned glass.

Garnish: orange slice

Mint Julep

The southern classic is making a huge comeback with hipsters. This mint-based delight has only one potential hazard: make sure you don't get a mint spring lodged in your teeth!

1 tsp. Sugar
4 Sprigs Mint
2 tsp. Water
3 oz. Bourbon

Muddle sugar, mint sprigs, and water in collins glass. Add bourbon with ice, then stir. Serve with short straws. *Garnish*: mint sprig

"SARABAR"
HOTEL SARASOTA COCKTAIL LOUNGE
SARASOTA, FLORIDA

RUM

Daydreams are made of Caribbean beaches, where the sun beams down on you while you are relaxing on a beach chair with a rum cocktail in your hand, or maybe a Mai Tai, Cuba Libre, or Piña Colada. Legend has it that rum was invented in Daiquiri, Cuba, in 1898 to combat a malaria outbreak. This trend to use rum as a medicinal "cure" continued with the U.S. settlers, who didn't have the means for doctor visits. That's one classic home remedy! Distilled and fermented from molasses and produced in the islands of the Caribbean, rum is most often 80-proof liquor, either dark or light in color. The exception is 151-proof rum—not for amateurs or the faint of heart.

Bacardi Cocktail

2 oz. Bacardi Light Rum

1 oz. Lime Juice

1 tsp. Grenadine

Combine ingredients in shaker with ice, shake, then strain into chilled cocktail glass.

Beachcomber

2 oz. Light Rum

$^1/_2$ oz. Triple Sec

$^1/_2$ oz. Lime Juice

2 tsp. Sugar

Combine ingredients in shaker with ice, shake, then strain into chilled cocktail glass.
Garnish: lime wedge

Continental

2 oz. Light Rum

1 oz. Crème de Menthe (green)

1 oz. Lime Juice

1 tsp. Sugar

Combine ingredients in shaker with ice, shake, then strain into chilled cocktail glass.
Garnish: lemon twist

Cuba Libre

$^1/_2$ oz. Lime Juice

2 oz. Light Rum

Cola

Combine lime juice and rum in highball glass. Add ice and fill with cola. *Garnish*: lime wedge

Cuban Cocktail

2 oz. Light Rum

$^{1}/_{2}$ oz. Lime Juice

1 tsp. Sugar

Combine ingredients in shaker with ice, shake, then strain into chilled cocktail glass.

Garnish: lemon twist

COCKTAILS ANYONE?

Daiquiri

We're not talking about those brain-freeze induc-ing frozen daiquiris here. Your classic cocktail Daiquiri is a straight up beautiful blend of liquor and sugar.

1 1/2 oz. Light Rum
1 oz. Lime Juice
1 tsp. Sugar

Combine ingredients in shaker with ice, shake, then strain into chilled cocktail glass.

Hurricane

1 oz. Light Rum
1 oz. Dark Rum
1/2 oz. Passion Fruit Syrup
1/2 oz. Lime Juice

Combine ingredients in shaker with ice, shake, then strain into chilled cocktail glass.

Mai Tai

"Mai tai—roa aé."

Say that three times after drinking a few strong Mai Tais. Translated from Tahitian, it means "Out of this world—the best." The Mai Tai was created in 1944 by Trader Vic (né Victor Bergeron).

2 oz. Light Rum
1 oz. Triple Sec
1/2 tsp. Sugar
1/2 oz. Orgeat Syrup
1 tbsp. Grenadine
1/2 oz. Lime Juice

Combine ingredients in shaker with ice, shake, then strain into ice-filled old-fashioned glass. Serve with straws. *Garnish*: cherry speared to pineapple wedge

Piña Colada

3 oz. Light Rum

4 oz. Pineapple Juice

1 1/2 oz. Coconut Milk

Combine ingredients with 2 cups crushed
ice in blender and blend at high speed.
Strain into collins glass and serve with straw.
Garnish: pineapple wedge and cherry

Planter's Punch

2 oz. Lime Juice

2 tsp. Sugar

2 oz. Club Soda

2 1/2 oz. Light Rum

2 dashes Bitters

1/2 tsp. Grenadine

Combine lime juice, sugar, and club soda in mixing glass with ice, stir, and strain into ice-filled
collins glass. Add rum and bitters, stir, and top
with grenadine. Serve with straw. *Garnish*: lemon,
orange, and pineapple slices and cherry

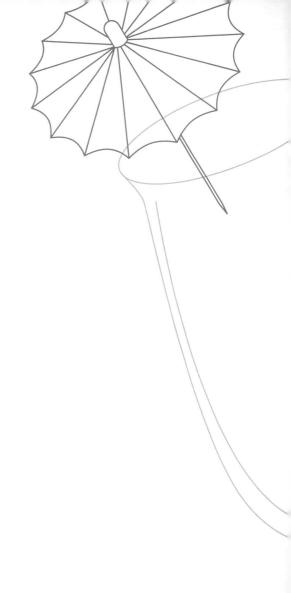

XYZ

1 oz. Rum

1 oz. Triple Sec

1/2 oz. Lemon Juice

Combine ingredients in shaker with ice, shake, then strain into chilled cocktail glass.

Zombie

2 1/2 oz. Light Rum

1/2 oz. 151-proof Rum

1 oz. Jamaican Rum

1/2 oz. Apricot Brandy

1 oz. Lime Juice

2 oz. Orange Juice

1 oz. Pineapple Juice

1 tsp. Sugar

Combine ingredients in blender with 1 cup crushed ice and blend for 1 minute at low speed. Strain into highball glass and serve with straw. *Garnish*: pineapple wedge, cherry, and fresh mint

When Your Spirit LAGS take a SWIG at SWAG'S

BRANDY

At once a delicious after-dinner drink and cooking ingredient, brandy can be traced way back to the early sixteenth century. An entrepreneurial Dutch trader boiled wine to remove the water (in order to ship the wine in sparse cargo space), then upon arrival added water back to the wine. This new spirit was referred to as "burnt wine," or *brandewijn* in Dutch. Years later, brandy was produced the way it's also made today, distilled from grapes or other fruit juice. Among the several different categories of brandies, the best are cognac and armagnac—both produced only in France in the regions whose names they bear. Additionally there are numerous fruit brandies (blackberry, apricot, apple, etc.), American brandies (produced in California), and European brandies. Take it to the next level at your upcoming cocktail party—serve fine brandy in snifters and heat the glasses with your hand. Warm is best when serving brandy straight up!

Apricot Cocktail

1 1/2 oz. Apricot Brandy

1/2 oz. Gin

1/2 oz. Orange Juice

1/2 oz. Lemon Juice

Combine ingredients in shaker with ice, shake, then strain into chilled cocktail glass.

Bombay Cocktail

1 oz. Brandy

1/2 oz. Dry Vermouth

1/2 oz. Sweet Vermouth

1/2 tsp. Triple Sec

1/4 tsp. Anisette

Combine ingredients in shaker with ice, shake, then strain into chilled cocktail glass.

Bosom Caresser

1 oz. Brandy

1/2 oz. Triple Sec

1 oz. Madeira

Combine ingredients in shaker with ice, shake, then strain into chilled cocktail glass.

Brandy Alexander

1 oz. Brandy

1 oz. Heavy Cream

1 oz. Crème de Cacao (dark)

Combine ingredients in shaker with ice, shake, then strain into chilled cocktail glass.

Brandy Crusta Cocktail

1 Lemon Wedge

1 tsp. Sugar

2 oz. Brandy

1 oz. Maraschino Liqueur

1/2 oz. Triple Sec

1 oz. Lemon Juice

Rub rim of collins glass with lemon wedge, then dip glass into sugar to coat rim. Shake brandy, maraschino liqueur, triple sec, and lemon juice with ice, then strain into glass. *Garnish*: orange slice

Deauville Cocktail

1/2 oz. Brandy

1/2 oz. Apple Brandy

1/2 oz. Triple Sec

1/2 oz. Lemon Juice

Combine ingredients in shaker with ice, shake, then strain into chilled cocktail glass.

East India Cocktail

1 1/2 oz. Brandy

1/2 oz. Triple Sec

1 oz. Pineapple Juice

1 dash Angostura Bitters

Combine ingredients in shaker with ice, shake, then strain into chilled cocktail glass.

Jack Rose Cocktail

1 1/2 oz. Apple Brandy

1/2 oz. Lime Juice

1/2 tsp. Grenadine

Combine ingredients in shaker with ice, shake, then strain into chilled cocktail glass.

Royal Smile Cocktail

1 oz. Apple Brandy

1 oz. Gin

1/2 oz. Lemon Juice

1 tsp. Grenadine

Combine ingredients in mixing glass with ice, stir, then strain into chilled cocktail glass.

Sidecar

1 oz. Brandy

1 oz. Triple Sec

1 oz. Lemon Juice

Combine ingredients in shaker with ice, shake, then strain into chilled cocktail glass.

Stinger

2 oz. Brandy

1/2 oz. Crème de Menthe (white)

Combine ingredients in shaker with ice, shake, then strain into chilled cocktail glass.

Third Rail

1 oz. Brandy

1 oz. Apple Brandy

3/4 oz. Light Rum

1/4 tsp. Anisette

Combine ingredients in shaker with ice, shake, then strain into chilled cocktail glass.

Whip Cocktail

1 1/2 oz. Brandy

1/2 oz. Dry Vermouth

1/2 oz. Sweet Vermouth

1/2 oz. Triple Sec

1/4 tsp. Anisette

Combine ingredients in mixing glass with ice, stir, then strain into chilled cocktail glass.

Widow's Kiss

1 oz. Brandy

1/2 oz. Benedictine

1/2 oz. Yellow Chartreuse

1 dash Bitters

Combine ingredients in shaker with ice, shake, then strain into chilled cocktail glass.

TEQUILA

Lick the salt off your hand, down the tequila, suck on a lime, and enjoy the little burn in your stomach and the newfound bounce in your step . . . oh the beauty of the perfect tequila shot! As well as being a popular shooter, tequila has made its way into the list of classic cocktails, mainly by way of the beloved margarita. Distilled from fermented blue agave plants, tequila is made exclusively across the border in Mexico. There are various "levels" of this spirit; the top of the line, so-called super-premiums or premiums, are produced wholly by blue agave. The commonly known tequilas (many bottled in the United States) contain only about 51 percent blue agave sugar combined with sugarcane alcohol. These tequilas can be blamed for those horrible hangovers the next day; so, if you're planning a cocktail party for friends—do them a favor and serve 100 percent blue agave tequila.

Brave Bull

2 oz. Tequila

1 oz. Kahlúa

Combine ingredients in mixing glass with ice,
stir, then strain into ice-filled old-fashioned glass.

Margarita

1 Lime Wedge

Salt

2 oz. Tequila

1 oz. Triple Sec

2 oz. Lime Juice

Rub lime wedge on rim of cocktail glass, then dip
glass in salt to coat rim. Shake tequila, triple sec,
and lime juice with ice, then strain into glass.
Garnish: lime wedge

Matador

1 1/2 oz. Tequila

3 oz. Pineapple Juice

1 oz. Lime Juice

Combine ingredients in shaker with ice, shake, then strain into sour glass.

Shady Lady

2 oz. Tequila

1 oz. Melon Liqueur

5 oz. Grapefruit Juice

Combine ingredients in mixing glass with ice, stir, then strain into ice-filled highball glass.
Garnish: lime and cherry

Silk Stockings

2 oz. Tequila

1 oz. Crème de Cacao

1 tsp. Chambord

2 oz. Heavy Cream

Cinnamon

Combine ingredients in shaker with ice, shake, then strain into chilled cocktail glass. Sprinkle dash cinnamon on top.

Tequila Sunrise

2 oz. Tequila

4 oz. Orange Juice

1 oz. Grenadine

Combine tequila and orange juice in mixing glass with ice, stir, then strain into ice-filled highball glass. Pour in grenadine.

Toreador

2 oz. Tequila

1 oz. Crème de Cacao (dark)

1 oz. Light Cream

¹/₄ tsp. Cocoa Powder

Combine tequila, crème de cacao, and cream in shaker with ice, shake, then strain into chilled cocktail glass. Sprinkle dash cocoa powder on top.

Viva Villa

1 Lime Wedge

Salt

2 oz. Tequila

1 oz. Lime Juice

1 tsp. Sugar

Rub rim of old-fashioned glass with lime wedge, then dip glass into salt to coat rim. Shake tequila, lime juice, and sugar with ice, then strain into glass.

LIQUEURS, CORDIALS, Etc.

Skip dessert! Indulge your sweet tooth with these sophisticated cocktails: Amaretto Sour, Grasshopper, and Toasted Almond. Liqueurs (or cordials, as they are also called) are sweetened liquors flavored with chocolate, fruits, nuts and spices, among other things, to create their unique taste. Serve a liqueur at your next dinner party as an after-dinner treat, or create a party around a sweet cordial.

Amaretto Sour

1 1/2 oz. Amaretto

3/4 oz. Lemon Juice

Blend ingredients with ice, then strain into sour glass. *Garnish*: orange slice and cherry

Golden Cadillac

1 oz. Galliano

2 oz. Crème de Cacao (white)

1 oz. Light Cream

Blend ingredients with ice at low speed for a short time, then strain into champagne flute.

Pink Squirrel

1 oz. Crème de Noyaux

$^3/_4$ oz. Crème de Cacao (white)

1 oz. Light Cream

Combine ingredients in shaker with ice, shake, then strain into chilled cocktail glass.

Ritz Fizz

Champagne

1 dash Blue Curaçao

1 dash Amaretto

1 dash Lemon Juice

Fill champagne flute with champagne. Add other ingredients and stir. *Garnish*: lemon twist

Grasshopper

1 oz. Crème de Menthe (green)

1 oz. Crème de Cacao (white)

1 oz. Light Cream

Combine ingredients in shaker with ice, shake, then strain into chilled cocktail glass.

Negroni

1 oz. Sweet Vermouth

1 oz. Gin

1 oz. Campari

Combine ingredients in shaker with ice, shake, then strain into chilled cocktail glass. *Garnish*: lemon twist

Sloe Gin Fizz

2 oz. Sloe Gin

1 oz. Lemon Juice

1 tsp. Sugar

1/2 oz. Club Soda

Combine sloe gin, lemon juice, and sugar in shaker with ice, shake, then strain into ice-filled highball glass. Top with club soda and stir. *Garnish*: lemon slice

Toasted Almond

1 1/2 oz. Kahlúa

1 oz. Amaretto

1/2 oz. Light Cream

Combine ingredients in shaker with ice, shake, then strain into ice-filled old-fashioned glass.

Wine and

CHAMPAGNE

Cocktails

Wine and champagne are wonderful on their own, but can also be a delightful blend in a mixed drink. Moreover, wine and champagne cocktails have an extra elegance to them, as most are served in a glamorous champagne flute or cocktail glass. Grapes are the exclusive ingredients of wine; and champagne is wine that's made using the *méthode champenoise*, a special fermentation and bottling process. Truth be told, only champagnes produced in the Champagne region of France can have that name. Otherwise, they're sparkling wines. White wines and champagne should be kept cold; red wines are stored at room temperature.

Adonis Cocktail

2 oz. Dry Sherry

1 oz. Sweet Vermouth

1 dash Orange Bitters

Combine ingredients in mixing glass with ice, stir, then strain into chilled cocktail glass.

Americano

2 oz. Campari

2 oz. Sweet Vermouth

Club Soda

Pour Campari and sweet vermouth into ice-filled highball glass. Fill glass with club soda, then stir.

Garnish: lemon twist

Bamboo Cocktail

2 oz. Dry Sherry

$^1/_2$ oz. Dry Vermouth

1 dash Orange Bitters

Combine ingredients in mixing glass with ice, stir, then strain into chilled cocktail glass.

Bellini

3 oz. Peach Nectar

$^1/_2$ oz. Lemon Juice

Champagne

Combine nectar and juice in shaker with ice, shake, then strain into champagne flute. Fill with champagne.

Champagne Cocktail

1 Sugar Cube

2 dashes Angostura Bitters

Champagne

Put sugar cube and bitters at bottom of champagne flute. Fill with champagne. *Garnish*: lemon twist

Kir

2 oz. Crème de Cassis

White Wine

Pour crème de cassis into ice-filled wineglass. Fill with white wine and stir. *Garnish*: lemon twist

Kir Royale

2 oz. Crème de Cassis

Champagne

Stir crème de cassis with ice in mixing glass, then strain into champagne glass. Fill with champagne.

Mimosa

3 oz. Champagne

3 oz. Chilled Fresh Orange Juice

Fill champagne flute half full with orange juice, top with champagne, and stir.

Reform Cocktail

2 oz. Dry Sherry

1 oz. Dry Vermouth

1 dash Orange Bitters

Combine ingredients in mixing glass with ice, stir, then strain into chilled cocktail glass. *Garnish*: cherry

Sanctuary

2 oz. Dubonnet Rouge

1 oz. Triple Sec

1 oz. Amer Picon

Combine ingredients in mixing glass with ice, stir, then strain into chilled cocktail glass. *Garnish*: lemon twist

TOPS IN TAPS

ACROSS FROM CITY HALL
Rockford, Ill.

TOPS TAPS

Theme
PARTIES

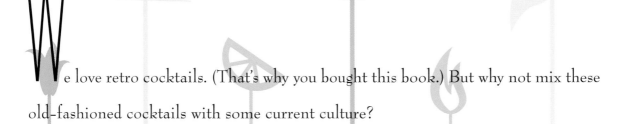

We love retro cocktails. (That's why you bought this book.) But why not mix these old-fashioned cocktails with some current culture?

The "Cocktail" Party

OK, the movie is so cheesy, but, hey, it's a cocktail classic! Rent the movie *Cocktail*, invite some friends over, and start mixing the drinks. You too can be inspired by a young Tom Cruise learning how to throw bottles in the air and showing off in front of female customers. If you can't bear the terrible dialogue, turn the volume down on the movie and up on your stereo with some classic '80s music (Duran Duran, INXS, Madonna—you get the picture). Since the movie takes place in the Caribbean, go with that theme by serving Mai Tais, Hurricanes, and Daiquiris. Complete the vibe with some leis for your guests, as well as some grass skirts for the more adventurous.

The "Austin Powers" Cocktail Party

This party can be combined with a Halloween party, where everyone has to dress up in '60s clothes. The host must show the first Austin Powers movie (the only really good one), and preferably, the host will dress up as either Austin or one of his babes. Martinis are all the rage for this party. Of course, serve the original basic martini, but also include the Cosmopolitan and fruity martinis (see the martini section of this book for ideas). You'll all be screaming, "Yeah, baby, yeah!"

The "Sex and the City" Party

Celebrate the revival of the classic martini with the four fabulous women from New York City! The women of *Sex* have single-handedly revived America's need to drink martinis, and drink a *lot* of them. Invite a group of friends over an hour before the show begins and serve classic martinis plus the new fruity popular versions. Note to male readers: don't think you won't enjoy this show (lots of hot babes and sex!).

The Anti-Superbowl Party

Football may be the most popular sport in America, but truth be told, there are some of us who just don't like watching men crash into each other in order to get ahold of a pigskin ball. Spend Superbowl Sunday afternoon with your fellow football haters sipping some serious retro cocktails. Since it's a cold January day, what better way to warm up than with a tequila-only cocktail party. Tequila Sunrises, Margaritas, Silk Stockings—all served to your guests with a knowing smile that they're living it up in style (while the rest of America is drinking beer and watching boring football).

The Singles Valentine's Day Party

Your single friends will thank you kindly for giving them something to do on this dreaded day. All drinks should be cherry red: Bloody Marys, Metropolitans, Aviations. Have every guest bring at least one single person he or she knows that he or she is not dating. That way you'll have lots of single minglers in attendance!

The Retro Happy Hour Party

Happy hour has long been thought of as a beer-only event. How about turning this idea on its head and serve classic cocktails at your party: Old-Fashioneds, martinis, Harvey Wallbangers, and Salty Dogs. You can also have cigars on hand for the wannabe rat packer boys. Play "oldies" music such as Sinatra, Tony Bennett, and Steve & Edie to enhance the lounge feel.

HAVE A HULA BIRTHDAY!

The Oscars Party

Oscar night is a great time to get some friends together to drink and socialize. Include an Oscar pool with your party invitation, and charge $5 to participate so everyone can afford it—a pool will give your party an extra fun atmosphere. Drinks you serve should be glamorous, as if they were being served on the red carpet: Bronx Cocktails, Manhattans, Cosmopolitans.

INDEX